FIRST FIE

ANIMAL
TRACKS
OF SOUTHERN AFRICA

Ostrich (page 15)

Burchell's zebra (page 41)

LOUIS LIEBENBERG

Contents

Key to African names:
A – Afrikaans; **S** – Sotho;
X – Xhosa; **Z** – Zulu.

*Broken branches, uprooted
trees and stripped tree bark
may serve as indicators of
an elephant's presence*

Struik Publishers
(a division of New Holland Publishing
(South Africa) (Pty) Ltd)
80 McKenzie Street, Cape Town,
8001 South Africa

New Holland Publishing is a member
of Johnnic Communications Ltd.
Visit us at **www.struik.co.za**
Log on to our photographic website
www.imagesofafrica.co.za
for an African experience.

First published in 2003

3 5 7 9 10 8 6 4

Editor: Katharina von Gerhardt
Designer: Lesley Mitchell

Reproduction by Hirt & Carter
Cape (Pty) Ltd
Printed and bound by Times Offset (M)
Sdn Bhd

ISBN: 1 86872 848 X

Introduction

The ability of Kalahari Bushmen trackers to interpret and understand the story behind each spoor is cultivated over a lifetime and developed to an exceptionally high degree. Men and women are able to identify the footprints of an individual person. They can identify the antelope they have shot from the rest of the herd, and have the ability to track down that specific animal. The animal's spoor may vary according to its age, mass, sex and condition. It may also have a unique way of walking or a particular habit that distinguishes it from other individuals of the same species.

People today are often not familiar with the immense variety of animal life that surrounds them, simply because most animals are rarely seen. To a 'spoor conscious' tracker, however, animal tracks may reveal the activities of a multitude of animals.

Leopards, for example, are very elusive and thus hardly ever seen. They have the uncanny ability to live near human settlements, often on the periphery of large cities. Finding leopard tracks in unexpected places can be exhilarating. Even if you never see the animal, the knowledge that it is there is immensely gratifying. By reconstructing animal movements from footprints, you may be able to visualise the actions of that animal. In this way a whole story may unfold – a story of what happened when no one was looking.

What is tracking?

The art of tracking involves each and every sign of an animal's presence that can be found in nature, including ground spoor, vegetation spoor, scent, feeding

Fine dust on this hard, dry ground will betray the leopard's passing through

signs, urine, faeces^G, saliva, pellets, territorial signs, paths and shelters, vocal and other auditory signs, incidental signs and skeletal remains.

Footprints provide the most detailed information on the identity, movements and activities of animals. The spoor illustrations in this book are exact studies made under ideal conditions – in other words, spoor that are clearly visible in mud or sand, and are not distorted. In reality, one will probably never find two animals with identical footprints.

One advantage of using ideal footprints is that it gives one a preconceived image, which makes it easier to identify imperfect tracks correctly, in conditions where the tracks may otherwise have been overlooked. Preconceived images play an important role in the recognition of patterns in nature. The 'danger' with them, however, is that one may misread random markings as spoor or one animal's spoor for another. One must therefore be careful not to be prejudiced and see what one would like to see.

Where and how to look

The clearest footprints are usually found in damp, slightly muddy earth, in wet sand, in a thin layer of loose dust on firm substrate, or in snow. Dirt roads and paths may have a thin layer of very fine dust on firm ground that can reveal the finest detail of the spoor.

Usually, however, footprints are partially obliterated, and one should walk up and down the trail to find the best imprints. Even if no clear footprints can be found, one can collect bits of

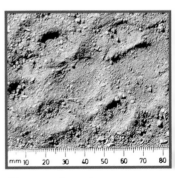

Civet spoor in sand

information by studying several footprints and piecing them together for an image of the complete spoor.

Keep in mind that footprints may be distorted owing to slipping and twisting of the feet on the ground. When an animal is walking or running on a slope, the feet may slip, so the spoor will appear elongated or warped. When trotting or running, the animal's mass is supported mainly on the toes and only part of the intermediate pads[G] may show, or, in the case of mongooses, the proximal pads[G] may not show at all. On hard ground padded toes may not show and only claw marks may be seen.

If the spoor could be that of several possible species, the distribution maps should be consulted to eliminate those that do not occur in that locality. Habitat and habits, such as sociability and daily rhythm, as well as feeding signs and faeces, should also be considered to narrow down the range of possibilities.

Skeletal remains can also provide the tracker with necessary clues

Spoor identification requires not only a great deal of knowledge, but also skill and experience. Although the inexperienced naturalist should be able to use this book to identify near-perfect spoor in ideal conditions, the accurate identification of imperfect spoor, especially in loose sand, may only be possible after considerable experience.

Note: Except where dimensions refer to 'shoulder height' (e.g. antelope), the 'length' for mammals always refers to the total length = (head + body + tail).

Wildlife in miniature

Even the smallest creatures leave tracks and signs. Dust on dirt roads and paths, as well as the silt in dried-up puddles, often shows the finest details of little tracks. If these tracks are found inside the track of a bigger animal, they may indicate the age of the tracks. For example, scorpions are nocturnal[G] so we know that if a scorpion track crossed the track of a bigger animal, the animal passed during the night or the day before.

Caterpillar

Millipede

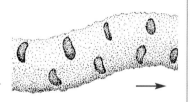

Dung beetle

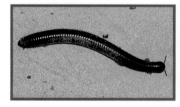

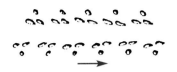

Termite

Grasshopper

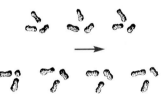

Tenebrionid beetle

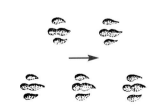

Scorpion

Snakes

Other names: slange (A), yin-yoka (Z), inyoka (X), dinoha (S)

Description: Long, legless reptiles found in all habitats. Vary in size, colour and markings.

Size: A blind snake may be only 20 cm long, while a python may reach 5 m in length.

Habitat: In southern Africa, 130 species are known to occur. Snakes are found in deserts and semi-arid areas, in forests, grass-lands and in the sea. All are cold-blooded. They are at their most active within their preferred temperature range of 20–32° C.

Habits: In hot weather, they move into the shade; in cold con-ditions snakes become sluggish; or may hibernate in extremely cold weather. They are highly sensitive to vibrations. Some snakes, like pythons, have heat receptors on their lips with which they can detect warm-blooded prey at a range of about one

Puff adder

metre, even in the darkest of nights. Vision is acute at a short range while poor at a distance.

Food: Feed on various animals, including small mammals, birds, reptiles, amphibians, insects and invertebrates, which are swallowed whole.

Spoor: Snakes use their bodies to move in either rectilinear (caterpillar-like) or undulatory fashion. **Rectilinear progression** – forward movement in a straight line – is characteristic of heavy-bodied snakes (pythons and adders). Belly muscles move the large ventral plates (belly scales) forward in alternate waves to enable the overlapping plate-edges to get a grip on uneven ground so that the body is drawn forward. With puff adders, there is usually a thin furrow down the middle of the trail where the snake has dragged the tip of its tail, and the ventral scales may leave clear markings. The spoor of puff adders and pythons can be distinguished by their ventral scales: the middle row of scales of the puff adder are almost as wide as the spoor itself; the python's are much narrower, so adjacent rows of scales also mark the spoor.

Undulatory or serpentine progression involves a series of sideways motions, 'rippling' from front to back, where each outward bend or curve of the snake's body pushes up against an uneven or rough surface and propels the snake forward. The sidewinding variation, in which the body is lifted from the ground in undulating motions, is characteristic of small, desert-living adders. The best time to follow snake spoor is in the early morning, before the wind obliterates the traces. To determine direction, study the way the earth has been pushed back.

Similar spoor: Could be confused with the tail spoor of a monitor or of a vervet monkey.

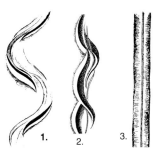

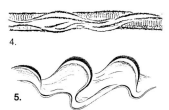

1. Typical snake 2. Puff adder (undulatory) 3. Puff adder (rectilinear) 4. Python (rectilinear) 5. Python (undulatory)

Land Tortoises

FAMILY TESTUDINIDAE

Other names: landskilpaaie (A), ufudu (Z), ufudo (X), dikgudu (S)

Description: Represented by 12 species in southern Africa. They are characterised by their dome-like shells and clawed feet.

Size: Ranges from the leopard tortoise (45 cm) to the speckled padloper (9 cm), the world's smallest.

Habitat: Need good ground cover for shelter in extreme temperatures.

Habits: Withdraw heads and limbs into the shell for protection. In cold periods, they seek sheltered places in which to hibernate. They incubate their eggs in the ground.

Food: Mainly plant matter. Some species eat snails, millipedes and other invertebrates; others gnaw bones and eat carnivore droppings for the calcium.

Spoor: Most land tortoises have five claws on the forefeet and four on the hind feet, however the greater padloper *Homopus femoralis* and the parrot-beaked tortoise *H. aerolatus* have four claws on the fore- and hind feet. Claws may be dragged through soft sand; only the claw marks may show on hard ground.

Angulate tortoise

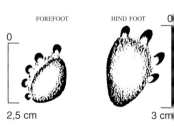

FOREFOOT   HIND FOOT   0

0

2,5 cm   3 cm

Similar spoor: Terrapins.

Passerines

Other names: sitvoëls (A)

Description: Passerines are small to medium-sized perching birds. The order is represented by more than 5 000 species worldwide, among them crows, ravens, sparrows, waxbills, canaries, buntings, wagtails, starlings, bulbuls, thrushes, chats and larks. They are represented in southern Africa by 29 families, most of which (about 80 per cent) are arboreal[G]. Size, habits and feeding patterns vary widely.

Cape Sparrow

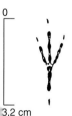

0

3,2 cm

Spoor: Three toes in front, one behind, adapted for perching. Do not have webbed toes.

Similar spoor: Other small birds that have back toes.

Longtailed Glossy Starling

Guineafowl

FAMILY NUMIDIDAE

Other names: tarentale (A), impangele (Z), impangele (X), kgaka (S)

Description: There are two species in this family in southern Africa, the Helmeted Guineafowl and the Crested Guineafowl.

Size: 50–58 cm.

Habitat: The Helmeted Guineafowl occurs in grassland, vleis, savanna, cultivated lands, edge of karoo scrub and bushveld. The Crested Guineafowl lives in montane, riparian and coastal forests.

Habits: Always in flocks.

Food: Feeds on a variety of seeds, bulbs, tubers, berries, insects, snails, ticks, millipedes and fallen grain.

Spoor: Three forward-pointing toes and an angled backward-pointing toe.

Helmeted Guineafowl

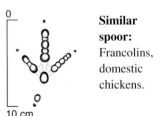

0

10 cm

Similar spoor: Francolins, domestic chickens.

Crested Guineafowl

Egyptian Goose

Alopochen aegyptiacus

Other names:
kolgans (A),
urhanisi (X)

Description: A large water
bird, brown above, greyish
below, with dark brown patches
around the eyes and on the cen-
tre of the breast, and a dark
brown collar on the neck. In
flight
the wings are white with
black primaries[G] and green
trailing edges.

Size: 63–73 cm.

Habitat: Most inland waters –
rivers, dams, floodplains, pans,
marshes; also estuaries, coastal
lakes and cultivated fields.

Habits: Highly gregarious[G].
Young chicks will follow their
mothers everywhere, and have
been known to jump and 'para-
chute' down from great heights,
from trees or buildings where
they have built nests, to be
with her.

Food: Grass and leaves, seeds,
grain, crop seedlings, aquatic
rhizomes[G]
and tubers.

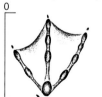

0

8 cm

Spoor: The
front toes
of the bird
are webbed,
the hind toes are reduced.

Similar spoor: Other ducks
and geese.

Kori Bustard

Ardeotis kori

Other names: gompou (A)

Description: Said to be the heaviest of all flying birds; greyish brown above, with a white belly, neck and a finely barred breast (though it looks grey from a distance). The head is slightly crested and the bill is long.

Size: 1,2–1,5 m.

Habitat: Open plains of the Karoo, highveld grassland, Kalahari sandveld, arid scrub, Namib Desert, lightly wooded savanna and bushveld.

Habits: Found singly or in pairs when breeding, otherwise gregarious^G, gathering in flocks of up to 40 or more individuals.

Food: Insects, small vertebrates, carrion^G, seeds and gum.

Spoor: Long legs with short, thick toes; the hind toe is absent.

Similar spoor: Ludwig and Denham's bustards.

Ostrich

Struthio camelus

Other names: volstruis (A), intshe (Z), inciniba (X), mpjhe (S)

Description: The world's largest living bird. Males are black with white wings while females are brownish grey.

Size: Up to 2 m in height.

Habitat: Bushveld to desert.

Habits: Found in flocks of 30–40 birds when not breeding. The eggs are unmistakable: large and ivory-coloured. They are laid in communal, earthen nests which are defended by a single male. Ostriches also produce copious amounts of mixed liquid and solid waste. Like that of all birds, urea[G] stains the droppings white. The call is a deep boom, not unlike the roar of a lion (for which it is often mistaken).

Food: Grass, berries, seeds, succulent[G] plants, small reptiles and insects.

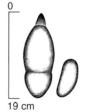

0

19 cm

Spoor: Legs are very long with only two toes.

Similar spoor: None, but at a glance can be confused with a human footprint.

Rats and mice

FAMILIES CRICETIDAE AND MURIDAE

Other names: muise & rotte (A), igundane (Z), ibuzi & impuku (X), dikgoto & dilegotlo (S)

Description: These rodents vary considerably in their habits and habitat.

Size: 10–80 cm (giant rat).

Habitat: Nests may be in underground burrows, in piles of vegetation, in rock crevices, or in holes in tree-trunks. Some species are terrestrial, others burrow. Most are nocturnal^G, although a few, like the striped mouse *Rhabdomys pumilio*, are active during the day.

Habit: There are both solitary and gregarious^G forms.

Food: Plant material, inverte-brates, small snakes and lizards, birds' eggs and nestlings.

Spoor: Four toes show in the fore footprints, five toes in the

Striped field mouse

hind footprints. When jumping, the hind prints appear ahead of the foreprints.

Actual size

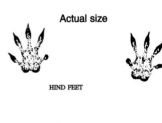

HIND FEET

FOREFEET

Similar spoor: Squirrels.

Springhare

Pedetes capensis

Other names: springhaas (A), indlulane, isandlulane (Z), tshipjane (S)

Description: With its short front legs, long powerful hind legs and long tail, the springhare bears a striking resemblance to a miniature kangaroo.

Size: Height 39 cm; tail 40 cm; mass 3,1 kg.

Habitat: Widespread.

Habits: Nocturnal[G]; congregates in scattered groups when feeding; usually feeds within 250 m of its burrow.

Food: Mainly grass.

Spoor: The springhare has five toes on the forefoot, with sharp, narrow, curved claws 18–20 mm in length over the curve. There are five toes on the hind feet, the first absent from the spoor, the second, third and fourth elongated (the third is the longest). The fifth claw, which is the shortest, does not mark in the spoor except when the animal sits up, in which case the whole hind foot, right back to the ankle, may show in the spoor. The marks of the front claws, used in excavation, can often be seen on the sides of a burrow, but seldom show in the spoor since the springhare usually moves on its hind feet – that is, it hops, holding the forelegs close to the body.

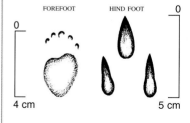

FOREFOOT   HIND FOOT

0

0

4 cm   5 cm

Similar spoor: None.

Porcupine

Hystrix africaeaustralis

Other names:
ystervark (A),
ingungumbane (Z),
incanda (X), noko (S)

Description: The largest African rodent, characterised by its erectile spines and black, brown and white quills.

Size: Length 84 cm; mass 18 kg.

Habitat: Most vegetation types.

Habits: Almost exclusively nocturnal[G]. Usually solitary, occasionally found in pairs or in groups comprising female and young. Defends itself by rattling its quills to intimidate its attacker or by reversing into the intruder to dislodge barbed quills.

Food: Diet includes bulbs, tubers, roots, wild fruit and carrion[G]; also gnaws the bark of trees.

Spoor: Five toes on the front foot, the first toe is reduced to a small stump without a claw. The other toes on the front feet have well-developed claws. Five toes on the hind foot, each with a claw. The fore- and hind feet each show three intermediate pads[G] and two proximal pads[G] in the spoor. The spoor also shows the marks of the quills, which are dragged behind the animal as it moves.

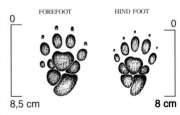

FOREFOOT HIND FOOT

0

8,5 cm   8 cm

Similar spoor: Honey badger.

Hares

FAMILY LEPORIDAE

Other names: hase (A),
unogwaja (Z), umvundla (X),
mofuli (S)

Description: Southern Africa
supports two species: the scrub
hare *Lepus saxatilis* has grizzled
buffy upperparts. The Cape hare
Lepus capensis is light buff in
colour, with black markings
in the southwestern Cape, and
a lighter grey with greyish
markings in Botswana.

Size: Length 45–60 cm; mass
1,5–4,5 kg.

Habitat: Distribution ranges
overlap. However, the Cape hare
prefers dry, open country (grassland plains) while the scrub hare
inhabits scrub or woodland.

Habits: Nocturnal[G] and solitary.
Lies up during the day in grass
clumps or under small bushes.

Food: Leaves, stems and rhizomes of dry, green grass. The
Cape hare favours areas with

Cape hare

short, green grass and fresh
green shoots.

Spoor: Leaves a characteristic
bounding trail – has thick hair
beneath the feet, so the pad
imprints are not well defined.
Four claws may show in the
spoor of the fore- and hind feet.

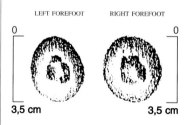

LEFT FOREFOOT   RIGHT FOREFOOT

0   0

3,5 cm   3,5 cm

Similar spoor: Rabbits.

Lesser Bushbaby

Galago moholi

Other names:
nagapie (A),
maselale-ntlwë (S)

Description: This primate has huge eyes and large ears. The upperparts are a light grey brown while the underparts are paler in colour.

Size: Length 30–40 cm; mass 120–210 g.

Habitat: Savanna woodland.

Habits: Nocturnal[G], solitary forager. Rests during the day in a family group consisting of two to seven individuals.

Food: Feeds mostly on insects (grasshoppers) as well as on tree sap and gum.

Spoor: Five digits on each foot, with soft, enlarged pads under the tip of each. Apart from the second digit of the hind foot, which has a curved grooming claw, each digit has a small nail. On the ground it moves by hopping on its hind legs, the forelimbs making no contact with the ground.

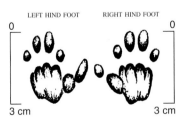

LEFT HIND FOOT   RIGHT HIND FOOT

3 cm   3 cm

Similar spoor: Thick-tailed bushbaby.

Vervet Monkey

Cercopithecus aethiops

Other names: blouaap (A), inkawu (Z), inkawu (X), khabo (S)

Description: Black-faced primate. Upperparts are grizzled while the underparts are whitish.

Size: Length 95–130 cm; mass 3,5–8,0 kg.

Habitat: Savanna woodland.

Habits: Diurnal[G]; active from dawn till mid-morning. It rests in a sheltered area until early in the afternoon (in hot weather), after which it continues foraging. Spends much of its time in trees searching for wild fruit, but also feeds on the ground. Troops comprise up to 20 members.

Food: Omnivorous[G], feeding on wild fruits, flowers, leaves, seed pods and insects.

Spoor: Thumb and big toe are fully opposable[G]. Each finger and toe has a nail. The feet are larger than the hands.

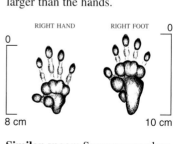

RIGHT HAND   RIGHT FOOT

8 cm   10 cm

Similar spoor: Samango monkey and small baboon.

Chacma Baboon

Papio ursinus

Other names: Kaapse bobbejaan (A), imfene (Z), imfene (X), tshwene (S)

Description: This is the largest southern African primate (after humans). Chacma baboons are formidable, especially the males: their canines^G can be longer than those of a lion.

Size: Length 1–1,6 m; mass 25–45 kg.

Habitat: Widely distributed; primarily savanna environment but also in mountainous areas and on forest fringes.

Habits: A gregarious^G species. Troops may number up to 100 individuals. Baboons are diurnal^G. They sleep on high krantzes or in trees with thick foliage at night.

Food: Omnivorous^G; diet includes grasses, seeds, roots, bulbs, leaves, flowers, wild fruits, pods and shoots. Turns over stones in search of insects, arachnids and slugs.

Spoor: The thumb and big toe are fully opposable^G; each finger and toe has a nail. The feet are twice as long as the hands.

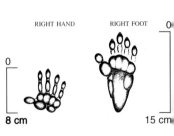

RIGHT HAND   RIGHT FOOT

0

0

8 cm   15 cm

Similar spoor: Monkeys.

Cape Clawless Otter

Aonyx capensis

Other names: groototter (A), intini/umthini (Z), intini (X), qibi/thene (S)

Description: Largest of Africa's otters. The upperparts range from light to very dark brown, the underparts are light in colour.

Size: Length 1,1–1,6 m; mass 10–18 kg.

Habitat: Aquatic. Needs fresh water, even in coastal areas.

Habits: Generally solitary, but also seen in pairs and family parties. Mainly crepuscular[G]. Latrines[G], which are situated near water, are characterised by crab-shell remains and fish scales. The droppings can be distinguished from those of the water mongoose whose scats[G] contain rodent fur and other items not normally eaten by otters. Identification is difficult where both species are feeding extensively on crabs alone. The water mongoose, however, leaves the carapace[G].

Food: Feeds mostly on crabs, frogs and fish.

Spoor: Five toes on the fore- and hind feet. The toes, adapted for feeling and grasping, have no claws on the forefeet and only rudimentary nails on the hind feet. In soft mud, the five toes, the inter-mediate pads[G] and the proximal pads[G] show clearly in the spoor.

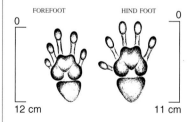

FOREFOOT HIND FOOT

0   0

12 cm   11 cm

Similar spoor: Spotted-necked otter but this animal has claws and webbing between its toes.

Honey Badger

Mellivora capensis

Other names:
ratel (A), insere (Z), magg (S)

Description: This stocky, short-legged badger has a broad, pale saddle which runs from above the eyes to the base of the tail, the colour contrasting with the black, lower parts of the body.

Size: Length 90–100 cm; mass 8–14 kg.

Habitat: The animal has a wide habitat tolerance – it is found everywhere except in true deserts.

Habits: Nocturnal[G]; generally solitary, though two or more individuals may hunt together. The animal is normally shy but it can be aggressive. When stressed, it may secrete a strong-smelling fluid.

Food: Omnivorous[G]; diet includes scorpions, spiders, mice, lizards, centipedes, grasshoppers, as well as small birds, snakes, berries, fruit, bee larvae and honey.

Spoor: Five toes on both fore- and hind feet. The claws on the front foot are elongated and powerful; the hind-foot claws are much shorter. The intermediate pads[G] are fused; a proximal pad[G] on the fore- and hind feet is characteristic of the spoor.

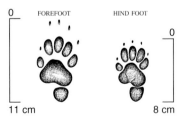

0   FOREFOOT   HIND FOOT
                                        0

11 cm   8 cm

Similar spoor: Porcupine.

Striped Polecat

Ictonyx striatus

Other names: stinkmuishond (A), iqaqa (Z), iqaqa (X), nakedi (S)

Description: A small animal with long, black and silky fur, and distinctive longitudinal white stripes on its body. The tail is mostly white.

Size: Length 57–67 cm; mass 0,6–1,4 kg

Habitat: The species has a wide habitat tolerance.

Habits: Nocturnal[G] and solitary, although one can occasionally see pairs and females with young. If cornered, the polecat will turn its hindquarters to the aggressor and eject a pungent secretion from its anal glands.

Food: Mainly insects and mice.

Spoor: Five toes on the fore- and hind feet. The claws on the fore-foot are strong, curved and long

(up to 18 mm over the curve); those of the hind feet are much shorter. All five toes and claws on the fore- and hind feet mark in the spoor. The proximal pad[G] on the forefoot does not show.

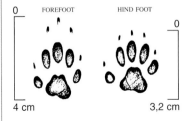

Similar spoor: Mongooses and weasels.

Small-spotted Genet

Genetta genetta

Other names: kleinkolmuskel-jaatkat (A), insimbi a ena mabala (Z), inyhwagi (X), tshipa (S)

Description: Distinguished from the large-spotted genet by a crest of black hair along the back, a longer and coarser coat, more black on the hind feet, darker body spots and (usually) a white-tipped tail.

Size: Length 86–100 cm; mass 1,5–2,6 kg.

Habitat: The more open areas of savanna woodland, dry grassland and dry vlei areas.

Habits: Nocturnal[G]; mainly solitary, but also found in pairs.

Food: Rodents, birds, reptiles, insects, spiders and scorpions.

Spoor: Identical to the spoor of the large-spotted genet. Five toes on fore- and hind feet; the first is set back and does not show in the footprints; nor do the sharp, curved, extendible claws.

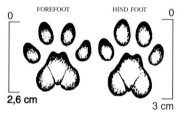

Similar spoor: Large-spotted genet, domestic and African wild cat.

African civet

Civettictis civetta

Other names: siwet (A), iqaqa (Z), inyhwagi (X), saparangaka (S)

Habits: Predominantly nocturnal^G; generally solitary.

Food: Omnivorous^G; diet includes insects, wild fruit, mice, reptiles, birds, amphibians, centipedes, millipedes, arachnids and carrion^G.

Spoor: Five toes on fore- and hind feet, but only four show in the spoor. The claws make clear marks.

Description: The greyish or whitish shaggy coat has black spots on the body, and black stripes on the tail and neck. The lower parts of the legs are black and the tail is bushy.

Size: Length 1,2–1,4 m; mass 9–15 kg.

Habitat: Well-watered savanna and forest.

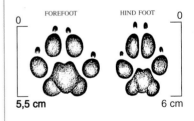

FOREFOOT   HIND FOOT

5,5 cm   6 cm

Similar spoor: The print of the hind foot can be confused with jackal spoor.

Suricate/Meerkat

Suricata suricatta

Other names: meerkat (A), ububhibhi (Z), igala (X), mosha (S)

Description: A small and attractive mongoose with conspicuous black rings around the eyes and a slender, tapering, black-tipped tail. Its general body colour is a light grizzled fawn with dark brown transverse bands on the back. The animal is commonly known as the meerkat.

Size: Length 45–55 cm; mass 6,2–9,6 kg.

Habitat: Occurs throughout southwestern arid zones.

Habits: Diurnal[G]; gregarious[G]; lives in warrens with several entrances, in colonies of up to 30 individuals.

Food: Mainly insects; also feed on scorpions, spiders, millipedes, centipedes, and small reptiles.

Spoor: Four toes on the fore- and hind feet. The claws on the front feet are strong and curved; the back ones are much shorter.

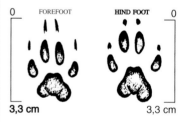

FOREFOOT   HIND FOOT

3,3 cm   3,3 cm

Similar spoor: All mongooses, especially yellow mongoose.

Water Mongoose

Atilax paludinosus

Other names: kommetjiegat-muishond (A), umvuzi (Z), umhlangala/vuzi (Z), motswitsi (S)

Description: A robust mongoose with a coarse, shaggy coat and tapering tail. Usually dark brown in colour.

Size: Length 80–100 cm; mass 2,5–5,5 kg.

Habitat: Associated with well-watered terrain – found near rivers, streams, marshes, swamps, vleis, dams and tidal estuaries.

Habits: Crepuscular^G. Normally a solitary species. Adult females may be accompanied by juveniles. Dry carapaces^G of crabs left on river banks are an indication of this mongoose's presence.

Food: Feeds on frogs, crabs, rodents, fish, insects, freshwater mussels and vegetable matter.

Spoor: Five toes on the fore- and hind feet. The first toe is small and shows in the spoor behind the intermediate pads^G. The other four toes are long and finger-like, and tend to splay. Claws on the front feet are stout and curved; those on the back are slightly longer. The proximal pad^G of the front foot, which may show in the spoor when the animal is moving slowly, may not mark at speed.

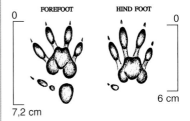

FOREFOOT   HIND FOOT
7,2 cm   6 cm

Similar spoor: All mongooses, especially large grey mongoose.

Black-backed Jackal

Canis mesomelas

Other names: rooijakkals (A), impungushe/khanka (Z), impungutye (X), phokobje (S)

Description: This jackal has a reddish-brown body, a black saddle on the back, and a bushy, black-tipped tail.

Size: Length 96–110 cm; mass 6–10 kg.

Habitat: Wide habitat tolerance.

Habits: Both diurnal[G] and nocturnal[G]; found alone, in pairs or family parties.

Food: Mainly carrion[G], but also small mammals such as rats and mice; as well as insects, vegetable matter, birds, reptiles, sun spiders, scorpions, centipedes and grass.

Spoor: Five toes on the forefoot; the first toe, which carries the dewclaw[G], is set well back and does not mark in the spoor. The hind feet have four toes. The claws are relatively short. Normally moves at a trot, leaving a trail in which both forefoot tracks lie on one side and both hind foot tracks on the other.

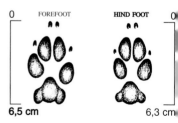

Similar spoor: Side-striped jackal, aardwolf, civet hind foot.

Bat-eared Fox

Otocyon megalotis

Other names:
bakoorjakkals (A),
udlamhloshana (Z),
impungutye (X),
motlhose (S)

Description: This attractive
animal has large, black-edged
ears, blackish legs and a bushy,
black-tipped tail. The overall
colour is a silvery grey.

Size: Length 75–90 cm; mass
3–5 kg.

Habitat: Especially associated
with open country within the
southwest arid and southern
savanna zones.

Habits: Diurnal[G] and nocturnal[G].

Food: Feeds on insects, in
particular harvester termites; also
scorpions, mice, reptiles, spiders,
millipedes as well as centipedes
and wild fruit. The holes, which
it digs when feeding, are characteristically narrow and deep.

Spoor: Five toes on the forefoot,
the first located far back so that it
does not mark in the spoor. The
claws on the forefeet are long
and slightly curved. Four toes on
the hind feet, with short claws.

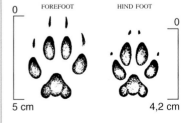

Similar spoor: Cape fox.

African Wild Dog

Lycaon pictus

Other names: wildehond (A), inkentshane (Z), ixhwili (X), mokoto/ tlalerwa (S)

Description: Its body is covered in a patchwork of black, yellow and white colours. It has large, rounded ears and a white-tipped bushy tail.

Size: Length 1,1–1,5 m; mass 20–30 kg.

Habitat: Open plains and open savanna woodland.

Habits: Adapted to living in packs of about 10–15 individuals, though pack size can number 50. Has very good eyesight. Generally active during daylight hours only – normally in the early morning and late afternoon.

Food: Mainly the smaller to medium-sized antelope; also hares and the young of the larger bovids[G].

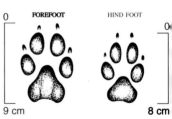

Spoor: Four toes on the fore- and hind feet, each carrying short, powerful claws.

Similar spoor: Domestic dog, cheetah.

Aardwolf

Proteles cristatus

Other names: maanhaarjakkals (A), isinci (Z), inyongci (X), thikgwi/thikhoi (S)

Description: The aardwolf is about the size of a jackal but hyaena-like in shape, with shoulders sloping down to the back legs. It has a thick mane on its back and a bushy, black-tipped tail. The body colour is yellowish brown, with vertical stripes.

Size: Length 84–100 cm; mass 6–11 kg.

Habitat: Wide variety of habitats, from semi-desert, karoo, to grassland and scrub, open savanna and woodlands. Does not occur in desert or forest.

Habits: Mostly nocturnalG; normally solitary, but may be found in pairs or family parties.

Food: Diet consists mainly of harvester termites; but it may also feed on spiders, rodents, millipedes and other insects.

Spoor: Five toes on the forefoot; the first toe is located high up and does not mark in the spoor. Four toes on the hind feet. The claws are narrow.

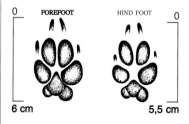

Similar spoor: Jackals.

Spotted Hyaena

Crocuta crocuta

Other names: gevlekte hiëna (A), impisi (Z), isandawane/ingcuka-cheya (X), phiri/sentawana/lefiritshwana (S)

Description: This carnivore has rounded ears and sloping hindquarters. The dull yellowish coat is dotted with irregular dark spots.

Size: Length 1,2–1,8 m; mass 60–80 kg.

Habitat: A savanna species associated with open plains, open woodland and semi-desert scrub.

Habits: Hyaenas live in groups or clansG, which are controlled by a dominant female. The territorial boundaries are carefully scent-marked with a creamy substance, which hyaenas secrete from their anal glands. Predominantly nocturnalG, but also active by day.

Food: Large or medium-sized ungulates, but will hunt or scavenge a wide range of prey.

Spoor: Four toes on the fore- and hind feet, each with a short, heavy claw. The spoor can be distinguished from that of the brown hyaena by the size difference between fore- and hind feet – a difference more marked in the brown hyaena.

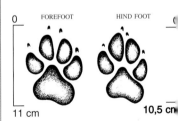

0   FOREFOOT   HIND FOOT

11 cm   10,5 cm

Similar spoor: Brown hyaena.

African Wild Cat

Felis lybica

Other names: vaalboskat (A), impaka (Z), ingada/ichataza (X), qwabi/tsetse (S)

Description: Looks like the domestic cat, but is slightly larger. Orange tint on back of ears, and stripes on forelegs are characteristic. The body colour ranges from greyish to ochre, with dark spots and stripes.

Size: Length 85–100 cm; mass 2,5–6 kg.

Habitat: Wide tolerance.

Habits: Nocturnal[G]; solitary. May be seen basking in the sun near the burrow. Like the domestic cat, it excavates a depression to defecate, and carefully covers the scats[G] by scraping with the front feet.

Food: Mainly rats and mice; also birds, reptiles, insects, spiders and small mammals such as hares, springhares and the young of small antelope.

Spoor: Footprints are similar in shape and size to those of the domestic cat.

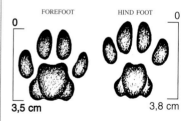

FOREFOOT   HIND FOOT

0   0

3,5 cm   3,8 cm

Similar spoor: Domestic cat, genets.

Cheetah

Acinonyx jubatus

Other names: jagluiperd (A), ingulule (Z), ihlosi (X), lengau/letlotse (S)

Description: Its body is designed for speed – it has a light build, long legs and a small head. The black 'tear marks' that run from the eye to the mouth are characteristic. Its spots are smaller and more rounded than the leopard's rosettes.

Size: Length 1,8–2,2 m; mass 40–60 kg.

Habitat: Wide range of habitats. It prefers open plains within savanna woodland.

Habits: Predominantly diurnalᴳ; at its most active around sunrise and sunset. The cheetah relies on its tremendous speed over relatively short distances to catch prey. Occurs in pairs or family parties of three or four. Solitary males are encountered occasionally.

Food: Carnivorousᴳ – feeds mainly on medium-sized antelope; also terrestrial birds, hares and porcupines.

Spoor: Unlike those of other cats, the cheetah's claws are not retractable. Longitudinal ridges beneath the intermediate padsᴳ act like tyre-treads to prevent skidding.

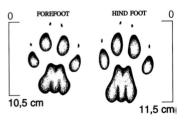

0   FOREFOOT   HIND FOOT   0

10,5 cm   11,5 cm

Similar spoor: Domestic dog, wild dog, leopard.

Leopard

Panthera pardus

Other names: luiperd (A), ingwe (Z), ihlosi (X), lengau (S)

Description: A thickset animal, with short, stocky legs, and a large head. Its body is a golden yellow colour, with distinct black, light-centred rosettes.

Size: Length 1,6–2,1 m; mass 20–90 kg.

Habitat: Wide tolerance.

Habits: Solitary, except during the mating season or when the female is accompanied by young. Mainly nocturnal^G, with some diurnal^G activity in undisturbed areas.

Food: Diet includes small to medium-sized antelope, on occasion larger mammals such as kudu and hartebeest as well as dassies, rats, mice, hares, birds, snakes, lizards, insects, scorpions, some of the smaller carnivores and occasionally baboons. Will also scavenge.

Spoor: Male's footprints are larger and proportionately broader than those of the female. The female's toes are more slender. The leopard extends its claws only when alarmed or charging.

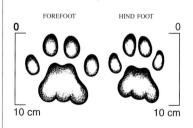

FOREFOOT   HIND FOOT

0   0

10 cm   10 cm

Similar spoor: Young or subadult lions, cheetah.

Lion

Panthera leo

Other names: leeu (A), ibhubesi (Z), ingonyama (X), tau (S)

Description: Largest of Africa's cats, sandy coloured; the males have a thick mane.

Size: Length 2,5–3,3 m; mass 110–225 kg.

Habitat: Wide tolerance.

Habits: Nocturnal^G and diurnal^G. Lions are highly social cats, and live and hunt in prides which may constitute a few individuals or above 30 individuals. Solitary males are ousted from prides. Solitary subadult males and females may also occur and tend to be nomadic. Lions scent-mark by spraying urine against shrubs, and at the same time make scrape marks on the ground.

Food: Mainly medium-sized to large antelopes, but will kill a wide variety of mammals, from giraffes to porcupines; also birds, reptiles and even insects.

Spoor: The male's footprints are larger and proportionately broader than those of the female; the female's toes are more slender than those of the male (a young male's footprints may be the same size as a female's but can be distinguished by the shape). The claws are extended when charging, and show in the spoor.

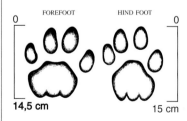

FOREFOOT   HIND FOOT

0   0

14,5 cm   15 cm

Similar spoor: Large male leopard.

Caracal

Felis caracal

Other names: rooikat (A), indabushe (Z), ingqawa (X), tnwane (S)

Description: A stocky cat with short limbs. The tail is bushy, and the ears have characteristic black tufts at their tips. The overall colour is a reddish tan.

Size: Length 70–110 cm; mass 7–19 kg.

Habitat: Associated with open savanna woodland, open grassland and vleis.

Habits: Mostly nocturnal[G]; solitary.

Food: Small and medium-sized prey, which includes monkeys, the young of the larger antelopes, dassies, birds and reptiles.

Spoor: Footprints are broad, and the indentation at the front of the intermediate pads[G] is prominent.

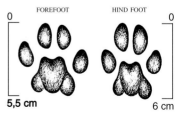

FOREFOOT HIND FOOT

0 0

5,5 cm 6 cm

Similar spoor: Serval.

White Rhinoceros

Ceratotherium simum

Other names: witrenoster (A), ubhejane omlophe (Z), umkhombe (X), tshukudu e molomo o sephara (S)

Description: An endangered species. Characteristic features are the square upper lip (animal also known as the 'square-lipped rhino') and the prominent hump above the shoulders. It is larger in size, and has a longer head than its cousin, the black ('hook-lipped') rhinoceros.

Size: Shoulder height 1,8 m; mass 1,4–2,3 tons.

Habitat: Areas of short grass with adequately thick bush cover and fairly flat terrain.

Habits: Grazes^G at night, in the morning, in the late afternoon and in the evening, resting at intervals for a few hours. During the heat of the day it rests in shaded areas. Occurs in small groups consisting of a dominant bull, subordinate bulls, cows and their offspring.

Food: Grass.

Spoor: Three toes, each with a broad, stout nail, on the fore- and hind feet. The nails are proportionately bigger, and gaps between them smaller than those of the black rhinoceros. The spoor of an adult is bigger. Cushioned pads on the soles of the feet show a mosaic of irregular cracks – a random pattern from which one can identify individuals.

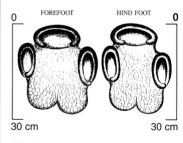

FOREFOOT   HIND FOOT

0   0

30 cm   30 cm

Similar spoor: Black rhino.

Burchell's Zebra

Equus burchelli

Other names: bontsebra (A), indube (Z), iqwarshe (X), pitsi ya naha (S)

Description: This common relative of the horse can be distinguished from the Cape mountain zebra by the yellowish or greyish shadow stripes between the black markings on the hindquarters, and also by the absence of a 'grid-iron' pattern on top of the rump.

Size: Shoulder height 1,3 m; mass 290–340 kg.

Habitat: Favours open woodland, open scrub and grassland.

Habits: Active by day. Gregarious^G; lives in small family units.

Food: A grazer^G, but will sometimes feed on herbs.

Spoor: Hoof-prints are similar in shape to, but much smaller than, those of adult horses, larger than those of domestic donkeys.

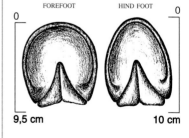

FOREFOOT   HIND FOOT

9,5 cm   10 cm

Similar spoor: Mountain zebras and donkeys.

Hippopotamus

Hippopotamus amphibius

Other names: seekoei (A), imvubu (Z), imvubu (X), kubu (S)

Description: This huge, barrel-shaped animal is well adapted to its aquatic life: eyes, nose and ears all protrude from the water when the rest of the animal is submerged.

Size: Shoulder height 1,5 m; mass 1–2 tons.

Habitat: Needs water in which it can totally submerge itself.

Habits: Nocturnal^G feeder; rests by day. Gregarious^G; occurs in herds (or schools), usually of between 10 and 15 individuals. Hippos tend to use established routes on dry land, the ground eventually being worn deeply into narrow paths. These are grooved on either side by the feet, leaving a narrow, raised central ridge of loose soil. Territories are marked by piles of faeces^G, which the hippo scatters over a bush or stone by flicking its tail from side to side. Can be aggressive if provoked, especially solitary bulls, or cows with calves.

Food: Grass.

Spoor: Has four toes, each with a heavy broad nail, on the fore- and hind feet.

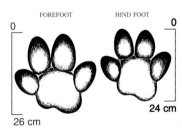

FOREFOOT   HIND FOOT

0   0

24 cm

26 cm

Similar spoor: None.

Giraffe

Giraffa camelopardalis

Other names:
kameelperd (A),
indlulaminthi (Z),
indlulamthi (X),
thuhlo (S)

Description: The world's tallest animal. There are several African varieties, each with a distinctive reticulate pattern. The head has horny projections. A long tongue enables the giraffe to strip the leaves off acacias; the viscous saliva it produces helps it to swallow the thorns. The animal defends itself by kicking. It can reach speeds of up to 60 km/h.

Size: Shoulder height 3,9–5,2 m; mass 970–1 400 kg.

Habitat: Dry savanna ranging from scrub to woodland. Often seen in company with zebra and wildebeest.

Habits: Predominantly diurnal[G]. Occurs singly, or in loose herds comprising females and young, bachelors or both. When fighting, two males stand side on and swing their long necks in wide arcs, aiming to hit the opponent's neck with the head and the neck.

Food: Browser[G]; favours acacia leaves and flowers.

Spoor: Footprints are much larger and longer than those of other cloven-hoofed animals.

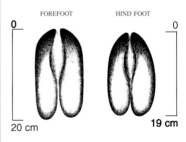

FOREFOOT   HIND FOOT

0   0

20 cm   19 cm

Similar spoor: None.

Warthog

Phacochoerus aethiopicus

Other names: vlakvark (A), indlovudalana/intibane (Z), ingulube (X), kolobe/mokhesi (S)

Description: An unmistakable animal with its characteristic tusks and wart-like facial protuberances. The skin is the colour of the local soil due to dust-bathing and rolling.

Size: Shoulder height 70 cm; mass 60–105 kg.

Habitat: Grassland, floodplains, vleis and other open areas, including open woodland.

Habits: Diurnal^G. Groups, called 'sounders', consist of an adult male, adult female and her offspring. Maternity and bachelor groups, and solitary individuals, are also found. Often wallows in mud and is prone to rubbing itself against any convenient object.

Food: Generally herbivorous, feeds on the rhizomes^G of grasses, sedges, herbs, shrubs and wild fruits.

Spoor: Hooves are narrower than those of bushpigs; the dewclaws^G usually mark clearly in the spoor.

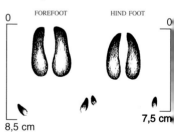

Similar spoor: Bushpig.

Elephant

Loxodonta africana

Other names:
olifant (A), indlovu
(Z), indlovu (X),
tlou (S)

Description: The world's largest
living land mammal. The trunk is
used for gathering food, drink-
ing, smelling, trumpeting,
breathing and as a weapon. Both
sexes have tusks.

Size: Shoulder height from 2,5–
4 m; mass from 2,8–6,3 tons.

Habitat: Wide habitat tolerance.

Habits: Family groups comprise
an adult female (matriarch[G]) with
her offspring or a number of
closely related females with their
offspring. Bulls join the herds
only when a female is in oestrus[G].
Elephants can be destructive when
feeding, uprooting trees or break-
ing branches to get at young
foliage. They dig holes in river
banks to drink filtered water.

Food: Browses[G] and grazes[G].

Spoor: Five hoofed toes on the
front feet and four on the hind.
The underfeet have a thick layer
of cartilage[G], enabling the elephant to move quietly. The horny
soles of the feet are cracked on
the surface, the mosaic of cracks
marking in the spoor. These
cracks allow a tracker to identify
individual elephants. The front
feet are rounder and larger than
the hindfeet.

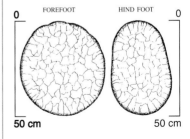

FOREFOOT · HIND FOOT

0 · 0

50 cm · 50 cm

Similar spoor: None.

Antbear (Aardvark)

Orycteropus afer

Other names:
erdvark (A),
isambane (Z),
thakadu (S)

Description: This singular animal
has a rounded back, pinkish
skin, a long snout, tubular
ears and a thick, tapering tail.

Size: Length 1,4–1,8 m; mass
40–70 kg.

Habitat: Wide tolerance.

Habits: Nocturnal[G] and solitary;
pairs and females with young
occur during the mating season.
Their excavated shelters often
have an extensive burrow system
with several entrances.

Food: Termites and ants.

Spoor: Four toes on the forefeet,
five on the hind, which are armed
with stout, broad claws. The front
footprints show three toes and
their claws: the first toe is absent,
and only the tip of the fifth claw

marks in the spoor. The hind footprint shows the three middle toes
and claws, and only the tips of the
first and fifth claws mark in the
spoor. The hind footprints usually
lie close behind or slightly overly-
ing the front ones.

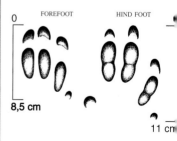

FOREFOOT   HIND FOOT

0

8,5 cm

11 cm

Similar spoor: None.

Common Duiker

Sylvicapra grimmia

Other names: gewone duiker (A), impunzi (X), impunzi (Z), phuti (S)

Description: A small antelope. Colour varies from a grizzled grey to a yellowish fawn. Has a characteristic black band running from the nose to the forehead. Males have short, straight horns.

Size: Shoulder height 50 cm; mass 18–21 kg.

Habitat: Wide tolerance; prefers savanna woodland.

Habits: Solitary; found in pairs when females are in oestrus[G]; also female with single young. Mainly active in the early morning, late afternoon, and at night. Uses secretions from its facial glands to mark its territory.

Food: Mostly a browser[G].

Spoor: Heart-shaped track.

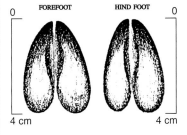

FOREFOOT   HIND FOOT
0   0
4 cm   4 cm

Similar spoor: Other duikers, steenbok.

Steenbok

Raphicerus campestris

Other names:
steenbok (A),
iqhina (Z),
itshabanqa (X),
thiane (S)

Habits: Solitary, except when the male is attending females in oestrus[G], or females are still with their young. Mainly diurnal[G]; active in the early morning and late afternoon.

Food: Both browses[G] and grazes[G].

Spoor: Sharp, narrow, pointed track.

Description: The upperparts of the steenbok are reddish brown, the underparts are white. The ears are very large and lined with white. Only the males have horns.

Size: Shoulder height 50 cm; mass 11 kg.

Habitat: Open grassland with cover; also in open woodland.

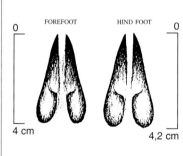

Similar spoor: Duikers and grysbok

Klipspringer

Oreotragus oreotragus

Other names: klipspringer (A), igogo (Z), kome/sekome (S)

Description: The colour of this agile antelope varies from speckled, yellowish brown to greyish brown. The coat has a coarse texture that blends in with the rocks among which it lives. Only the males have horns.

Size: Shoulder height 60 cm; mass 10–13 kg.

Habitat: Restricted to rocky and hilly habitats.

Habits: Found in pairs, singly, or in small family groups. Browses[G] or grazes[G] on flat ground surrounding its habitat, but if disturbed will run for rocky shelter. Active in the early morning and late afternoon. Scent-marks by smearing a black, tarry secretion from its facial glands onto twigs.

Food: Predominantly a browser[G].

Spoor: Walks on the tips of its hooves, which have long, narrow soles and blunt, rounded tips. The rounded hooves are an adaptation to the rocky terrain it inhabits.

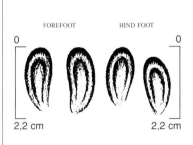

FOREFOOT   HIND FOOT

0   0

2,2 cm   2,2 cm

Similar spoor: None.

Springbok

Antidorcas marsupialis

Other names: springbok (A), insephe (Z), ibhadi (X), tshepe (S)

Description: This antelope has a cinnamon-brown back with a broad, reddish brown horizontal band separating the upperparts from the white underparts. Both sexes carry horns. The common name is derived from the way the animal springs with its back arched to expose a white ridge of hair. This is known as 'pronking', and is said to advertise its fitness.

Size: Shoulder height 75 cm; mass 37–41 kg.

Habitat: Arid area and grassland.

Habits: Gregarious G. Active in the early morning and late afternoon; some activity after dark.

Food: Both browses G and grazes G.

Spoor: Sharp, pointed track.

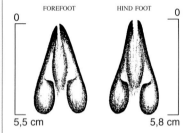

FOREFOOT   HIND FOOT

5,5 cm   5,8 cm

Similar spoor: Impala.

Kudu

Tragelaphus strepsiceros

Other names: koedoe (A), iqhudu (X), tholo (S)

Description: A large, fawn-grey antelope with 6–10 vertical white stripes on its sides. Only the males carry horns, which are long and deeply spiralled.

Size: Shoulder height 140–155 cm; mass 180–250 kg.

Habitat: Savanna woodland.

Habits: Gregarious^G; occurs in small herds, usually up to four individuals. Adult males may be solitary. Most active in the early morning and the late afternoon.

Food: A browser^G, but may eat fresh grass.

Spoor: The male's forefoot is broader than the female's.

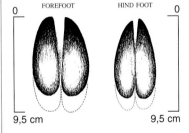

Similar spoor: Nyala.

Gemsbok

Oryx gazella

Other names:
gemsbok (A)

Description: A large antelope
with conspicuous black markings
on the body and face. The upperparts and flanks are a fawn-grey,
the underparts white with a broad,
dark-brown band in between.
Horns are straight, rapier-like,
the female's are more slender
than the male's.

Size: Shoulder height 1,2 m;
mass 210–240 kg.

Habitat: Open, arid country.

Habits: Gregarious[G]; occurs in
herds of up to 12 though solitary
males are common. Active during
early morning and late afternoon.

Food: Mainly a grazer[G]. The
gemsbok will dig in sand with its
front hooves for water, and for
succulent roots, rhizomes[G] and
bulbs. When defecating, the
territorial male adopts a
characteristically low posture,
which ensures that the faecal
pellets lie in a small pile and
so retain their odour longer.

Spoor: Sharp, pointed track with
straight edges.

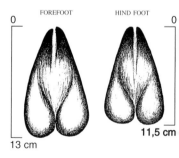

FOREFOOT
HIND FOOT
0
0
11,5 cm
13 cm

Similar spoor: Sable antelope,
red hartebeest, tsessebe.

Blue Wildebeest

Connochaetes taurinus

Other names:
blouwildebees (A),
inkonkoni (Z),
inkonkoni (X),
kgokong (S)

Description: Dark grey in
colour, with a mane of long
black hair. The tail ends in a tuft
of black hair. Both sexes carry
horns; the female's horns are
lighter in build than the male's.

Size: Shoulder height 1,5 m;
mass 250 kg.

Habitat: Associated with savanna
woodland and open grassland.

Habits: Gregarious^G; active in the
morning and afternoon. The male
marks his territories by dropping
onto his knees, rubbing a secretion
from his facial gland on the
ground, bushes and on tree trunks.

Food: A grazer^G.

Spoor: Triangular with blunted
points.

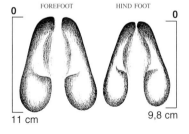

Similar spoor: Black wildebeest.

Eland

Taurotragus oryx

Other names: eland (A), impofu (Z), impofu (X), phofu/phohu (S)

Description: The largest of Africa's antelopes. Light rufous-fawn in colour, with narrow white stripes down the flanks. Both sexes carry horns; the male's horns are much heavier than the female's.

Size: Shoulder height 1,7 m; mass 450–700 kg.

Habitat: Wide tolerance.

Habits: Occurs in small herds, but occasionally in huge aggregations of more than 1 000. Active in mornings and afternoons.

Food: Mainly a browser^G, but will graze^G fresh, sprouting grass after fire.

Spoor: The hind foot is more elongated than that of the buffalo and of domestic cattle.

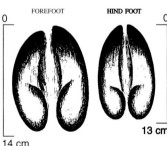

FOREFOOT   HIND FOOT

0   14 cm   0   13 cm

Similar spoor: Buffalo and domestic cattle.

Buffalo

Syncerus caffer

Other names:
buffel (A), inyathi
(Z), inyathi (X),
nari (S)

Description: A massive animal,
ox-like in appearance. Old males
are black; females have a tinge
of reddish brown. The curved
horns are huge in old adult
males. Females' horns are lighter
in build.

Size: Shoulder height 1,4 m;
mass 550–700 kg.

Habitat: Prefers open woodland
savanna and needs a plentiful
supply of grass, shade and water.

Habits: Gregarious[G]; occurs in
herds of up to several hundred.
Most active in the evening, at
night and in the morning.

Food: Mainly a grazer[G], but
also browses[G].

Spoor: Large, broad and circular
in shape. The dewclaws[G], which

show in soft mud, may not
always mark on hard ground.
The hind foot is not as elongated
as that of the eland.

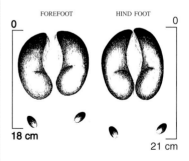

FOREFOOT   HIND FOOT

0   0

18 cm

21 cm

Similar spoor: Domestic cattle
and eland.

Glossary

Arboreal: Inhabiting trees.

Bovid: Of the family Bovinae (e.g. buffalo).

Browser: An animal that feeds mainly on trees and shrubs.

Canine teeth: Conical and pointed teeth in mammals, on each side of the upper and lower jaw.

Carapace: Shell (exoskeleton) on the back of the head and thorax of a crustacean.

Carnivorous: Feeding on meat.

Carrion: Disintegrated animal matter.

Cartilage: Tough, white flexible tissue between bones of animals.

Clan: Related individuals living in a family unit.

Crepuscular: Active at dusk or dawn.

Dewclaw: The claw of the second or fifth toe in mammals, usually high up at the back of the feet.

Diurnal: Active during the day.

Faeces: The waste matter that is discharged from the bowels.

Grazer: An animal that feeds mainly on grass.

Gregarious: Group-living.

Intermediate pads: The row of pads beneath the foot, just behind the toe pads.

Latrines: An area in which animals repeatedly defecate and urinate.

Matriarch: Dominant female in a group.

Nocturnal: Active during the night.

Oestrus: Short reproductive cycle in female mammals in absence of pregnancy.

Omnivorous: Feeding on plants and animals.

Opposable: The thumb of the primate hand can be placed against the other fingers, allowing for grasping and holding.

Primaries: The long feathers at the tip of a bird's wing.

Proximal pads: The pads on the foot that lie behind the intermediate pads, at the back of the foot.

Rhizome: Underground stem.

Scat: *see* faeces.

Succulent: Type of plant that stores water in its tissues; having a fleshy appearance.

Urea: Soluble colourless crystalline compound contained in urine.

Photographic credits

AB (Andrew Bannister), **AB/GI** (Anthony Bannister/Gallo Images), **AIC** (Africa Imagery.com), **CLB** (Colour Library), **DB** (Daryl and Sharna Balfour), **GD** (Gerhard Dreyer), **GI** (Gallo Images), **HPH** (HPH Photography), **HVDB** (Heinrich van den Berg), **HVH** (Hein von Hörsten), **IM** (Ian Michler), **KB** (Keith Begg), **LH** (Leonard Hoffmann),), **LVH** (Lanz von Hörsten), **ND** (Nigel Dennis), **PB** (Peter Blackwell), **PP** (Peter Pickford), **PVDB** (Philip van den Berg), **RM** (Rita Meyer), **SIL** (Struik Image Library), **TC** (Tony Camacho),.

All photographs by ND/SIL with the exception of the following: Front Cover: middle right (HVDB/HPH); bottom left (LVH/SIL); Back Cover: top left (PVDB/HPH); pg.2 (LVH/SIL); pg.5 (PP/SIL); pg.6 top right (LH/SIL), middle right (ND/AIC), bottom right (HVH/SIL); pg.7 (LH/SIL), except bottom right (TC/SIL); pg.8 (LH/SIL); pg.12 top right (PP/SIL); pg.14 (AB/SIL); pg.16 (LH/SIL); pg.17 (DB); pg.18 (TC/SIL); pg.19 (ND/AIC); pg.22 (LVH/SIL); pg.23 (GD/SIL); pg.24 (PVDB/HPH); pg.25 (AB/GI); pg.26 (ND/AIC); pg.27 (ND/AIC); pg. 29 (PVDB/HPH); pg.31 (IM/SIL); pg.33 (RM/SIL); pg.36 (LVH/SIL); pg.37 (IM/SIL); pg.38 (PP/SIL); pg.39 (HVDB/HPH); pg.40 (PP/SIL); pg.42 (CLB/SIL); pg.43 (CLB/SIL); pg.44 (LVH/SIL); pg.45 (HVH/SIL); pg.46 (ND/AIC); pg.47 (ND/AIC); pg.49 (PB/SIL); pg.50 (HVH/SIL); pg.51 (KB/SIL); pg.52 (DB/SIL).